Rhoda, Open Up!

Rev. Jacqueline Withers

Copyright © 2016 by Jacqueline Withers -
What He's Done for Me

Rhoda, Open Up! by Rev. Jacqueline Withers

Copyright © 2016 by Jacqueline Withers - What He's Done for Me. All rights reserved.

No part of this book may be reproduced in any written, electronic, recording, or photocopying without written permission of the publisher or author. The exception would be in the case of brief quotations embodied in the critical articles or reviews and pages where permission is specifically granted by the publisher or author.

Although every precaution has been taken to verify the accuracy of the information contained herein, the author and publisher assume no responsibility for any errors or omissions. No liability is assumed for damages that may result from the use of information contained within.

Cover Design: Germancreative at Fiverr.com
Publisher: What He's Done for Me
Editor: WordSharp.net
ISBN: 978-0-9974082-2-5

1) Spirituality 2) Spiritual Life 3) Christianity 4) Self-Help 5) Religion 6) Women

First Printing 2016

Printed in United States of America

Unless otherwise indicated, all Scripture references are taken from the Spirit-Filled Life® Bible copyright © 1991 by Thomas Nelson, Inc.

Scripture quotations marked KJV are from the Holy Bible, King James Version, © 1990 by Thomas Nelson, Inc.
Scripture quotations marked (CEV) are taken from the Contemporary English Version © 1995, American Life Bible Society.

Scripture taken from THE AMPLIFIED BIBLE, Old Testament copyright © 1965, 1987 by the Zondervan Corporation. The Amplified New Testament copyright ©1958, 1987 by The Lockman Foundation. Used by permission.

Scripture quotations marked (NLT) are taken from the Holy Bible, New Living Translation, copyright ©1996. Used by permission of Tyndale House Publishers, Inc., Wheaton, Illinois 60189. All rights reserved.

Scripture taken from the HOLY BIBLE, NEW INTERNATIONAL VERSION. Copyright 1973, 1978, 1984 by International Bible Society. Used by permission of Zondervan. All rights reserved.

About the Cover

The name *Rhoda* comes from the Greek isle of Rhodes. This isle got its name because of the roses. It's been called a flowery place throughout antiquity. Orange roses symbolize enthusiasm and desire, which Rhoda had. The orange-colored rose is closed to symbolize the fact that she didn't open the door.

Dedication

I dedicate this book to my son
Jonathan Corey
And my daughter
Olivia Janeel

*"I have no greater joy than to hear
that my children walk in the truth."*
1 John 1:4

PREFACE

I began writing this book well over ten years ago. During one of the times while reading in the book of Acts, Rhoda's story penetrated my heart. The question that came to mind was, "Why didn't she open the door?"

I have since preached on that subject, but couldn't seem to complete the book. I would be inspired to put the floppy disc, now flash drive, in the computer every few months. Then, I would start writing and soon lose the momentum. Year after year, even skipping a year once in a while. Finally, in 2013 I started again with a determination to finish this no matter what it cost.

There was an agent I had been communicating with from one of the large independent publishing companies who made me believe that it was time to get my book out. Thank God, for someone who agreed with me. I had arranged for him to call me one evening to could complete the transaction. I told him what time I'd be home from work and would wait for his call.

Sitting by the phone with my credit card in my hand, I prayed. "Lord if there is any reason I shouldn't do this, please speak now." I was also praying that nothing would interrupt me while on this call: "Protect this time from all emergencies, let no one else call me." No dinner, or beverages until this is over; I didn't want to have to go to the bathroom. My cellphone's battery was charged, even cleaned it off (like that was going to help me hear better). Years had passed waiting to do this and now was the day.

The phone never rang. After an hour of just sitting there, I finally dared to call someone to make sure my phone still worked. The person even called me back to be certain. No technical problems were found. I was crushed. What happened, God? Why didn't the agent call me? Of course, he wanted the sale as much as I wanted to publish this book. I took all the papers, the two home-made books I had printed, all my notes and shoved them into a box. It didn't matter if the pages were out of order because I was tired of this project. My feelings were hurt for the last time. In 2014 when a little inclination came to pull it out again, I decided if those pages came out of that box, it would be to shred. Later for Rhoda!

The following year, God revealed to me why He hadn't let me complete this book. There was something He was trying to reveal to me. I was Rhoda!

I heard, and recognized God's voice, yet hadn't learned the right way to respond. No one but God could have convinced me of this. Looking back over my life and the many times I didn't "get it" leads me to love God even more. It wasn't that He didn't want me to succeed, He did. He was willing, but I wasn't ready. Someone said that, *the teacher comes when the student is ready.*

Don't miss out on what this book is trying to show you. Try to see my experiences as God's way of speaking to you. He is still speaking, so why aren't you walking in the fullness of those things that He's revealing to you? The *Teacher* will come when you're ready to learn. This is the lesson He wants me to share with you.

Rev. Jacqueline Withers

ACKNOWLEDGEMENTS

The God who fearfully and wonderfully made me, fearfully and wonderfully saved me, and fearfully and wonderfully keeps me day-by-day gets all the glory for blessing me to write this book. There were many times I wanted to give up on my dream to write. Now, I understand why it took me so long to complete it.

I am truly thankful to Rev. Dr. George W. Maize, III who was my Pastor when I started this project. He never hesitated to call me an Author or Playwright.

I owe a debt of gratitude to Rev. Dr. Thelma L. Gattis. She accepted the role God gave her, as my mentor, for many years. Even when she takes off her Pastor's robe, and hangs it in the closet, you know from her life that she is dedicated to serving God. Others, who inspired me are:

My daughter Olivia J. Withers, whose prayers kept me lifted up before God. She is a witness of the power of God's grace and love. Her life demonstrates what it means to open up and let God lead.

Mrs. Norma Waithe, who always has an ear to listen, never judges and loves me in spite of my imperfections. She has been such a devoted friend and supporter of me and this project.

Other people who either assisted in editing, praying and supporting me are: Mrs. Tracey Taylor,

Mrs. Nana Withers, Mrs. Rosalyn Jackson, Rev. Maurice Daniels, Minister Lawrence Q. Alexander, Rev. Paula Davis, Rev. Mack Brandon, all the intercessors of Day Start, and Rev. Charles Washington. It would have been very difficult to complete this book without their help.

Finally, Damon "STEAM" Teacher Jones – I owe a very special thanks to you for allowing me to interview you. May God continue to reign over you and His blessings rain over your work so you'll bring forth a fruitful harvest to His glory.

Please access his websites and support this wonderful ministry.

www.steam-america.org

socksmovement.org

Contents

Preface i

Acknowlegements iv

Prologue vii

The Knock 1

Praying for a Change 9

The First Responders 35

Appearances 49

Don't Tell – Go Show 59

The Voice 69

Come In 83

Epilogue 97

Endnote 104

About the Author 107

Prologue

God speaks to us in various ways. In spite of our supposed intelligence and personal wisdom, He still speaks through His ministers. He also uses laypersons, family, friends, and even strangers to get a message to us. Occasionally, He even speaks to us through visions or dreams. Of course, the surest way, He uses is His written and living word, the Bible. He's talking to you right now.

We know how foolish, careless or simply, how sinful we can be; but our omnipotent God loves us. He knows our faults, yet provides our needs. We pray and sometimes fast, waiting for instruction or direction. He sees us in our poverty of spirit and shows us mercy by answering our prayers.

When we hear His voice or receive understanding, we are so filled with awe and gratitude. As the Shepherd, He will either knock on the door of our heart with a word of encouragement to inspire our spiritual growth or give revelation over something we've prayed about. Either way, you realize it's Him knocking and, saying - *this is the way, walk in it*.[1]

In some cases, we get so excited and can't hide it; we have to tell someone what God has said. We call our prayer partners, our friends and tell them that we've received a word from heaven. For the first time in years, we can't wait to get to church on Sunday. We sit there with great anticipation waiting for testimony time to share our great joy. Praise God for His grace and mercy. We thank Him for caring so much for us. We bless Him for leading us in the way we should go. I want to say, that *was* me.

What happens next? Our emotional high lasts a few days, and the feelings start to dissipate. The wonderment fades away, and we go back to our usual selves and habits. We all have a list of regrets because we only *intended* to obey. Somehow, we never did. If we check our journals, we may find that God has spoken to us about the same thing before. That's what I noticed in my journals.

How is it we let some excuse keep us from trusting God? Benjamin Franklin said, *"He that is good for making excuses is seldom good for anything else."*[2] God isn't trying to entertain us. None of us, regardless of our age, has the luxury of time on our side. It is crucial that we learn to listen and obey. Our salvation is nearer than when we first believed.

After the resurrection, the disciples were together in a room behind a locked door. Jesus suddenly appeared in that room without a knock, without waiting for anyone to answer. I haven't heard of Him doing that again. Now, He knocks and waits for us to open up and let Him in. Even in the parable of the shepherd, the porter or doorkeeper opened the door.[3]

What is hindering you from taking that bold

step to open the door of your heart? What will it take for you to get serious and adhere to His will? When are you going to let the word you hear change you? When are you going to apply the instructions that you received to your life? I want to help you learn what I've learned before another day of living purposefully passes by.

It is written of Rhoda, "*When she recognized Peter's voice, because of her gladness she did not open the gate, but ran in and announced that Peter stood before the gate.*" (Acts 12:14 NKJV)

Yes, like Rhoda (our title character), we have prayed and prayed.

Yes, like Rhoda, we heard and recognized the voice.

Yes, like Rhoda, we were overjoyed, but just like Rhoda, we walked away without opening the door. That was my story, until now.

Hear what the Spirit is saying to you. Then open up, let Him in and be blessed.

Chapter 1

THE KNOCK

It was about this time that King Herod arrested some who belonged to the church, intending to persecute them. He had James, the brother of John, put to death with the sword. When he saw that this met with approval among the Jews, he proceeded to seize Peter also. This happened during the Festival of Unleavened Bread. After arresting him, he put him in prison, handing him over to be guarded by four squads of four soldiers each. Herod intended to bring him out for public trial after the Passover.

So Peter was kept in prison, but the church was earnestly praying to God for him.

[13]Peter knocked at the outer entrance, and a servant named Rhoda came to answer the door. When she recognized Peter's voice, she was so overjoyed she ran back without opening it and exclaimed, "Peter is at the door!"

Acts 12:1-5, 13, 14 (NIV)

Rhoda, Open Up!

Ah, take a moment and picture this scene. The fearful yet faithful anxiously gathered at Mary's house to pray for their wellbeing and Peter's safety too. The death of Stephen caused many of "the way" to flee from the city (Acts 7:54-60). Herod Agrippa I was persecuting them to win favor with the Jews. It's easy to presume that the news of James' death, ordered by King Herod, now Peter's imprisonment, rattled their nerves; perhaps, even their faith. They did what every Christian should do in times of intense persecution - pray! They were likely in that room for several days crying out for God to deliver Peter. Their help could only come from the Lord.

> *Not Peter, Lord, we need him. He's our pastor, teacher, leader, and friend. We need his courage to strengthen us. Who else would be bold enough to proclaim to a multitude of devout Jewish men that Jesus is the Christ and tell them to repent? Oh, Lord don't let them take his life too. If he's killed who will take his place? Casting lots won't help us now; we need Peter.*

Rhoda was a servant[1] in the house, and was a fellow follower of Christ. She too was likely praying and crying out to God for Peter's release. The noise of their wails undoubtedly filled the room. Since Peter had just escaped from prison, it's simple to assume that his knock would have been soft. No banging on the door in the middle of the night at a house where the believers secretly gathered. Yes, Rhoda loved this leader of the faith, and her heart was also heavy with concern for all their lives. Still, she was the servant girl. Rhoda *heard* the knocking. The sound might have interrupted some other follower's concentration, but Rhoda, as a servant, her ears fine-tuned for any knock at the door, understood her duties. She was a slave of Christ; like Onesimus, she was still a slave. Demetrius K. Williams described the scene this way:

"While certain elements of this episode are comedic, it must be kept in mind that Rhoda is a stereotypical 'slave' as perceived in Greco-Roman culture."[2]

She was at Mary's house, where perhaps they gathered before to listen to Peter tell the stories he'd learned from Jesus Christ. She listened intently as he declared the good news of salvation. Her ears recognized his voice as well as that of her master. Believing his words, she received Jesus as her Savior. Now, she was with the others, the Apostles and disciples, praying for Peter's release.

Consequently, she arose from her position, bowed down in prayer, to do the humble work of a servant - answer the door. However, there was a problem. She didn't open the door.

We tell our children to, "See who it is" before they open the door. We have glass windows or peepholes, if not cameras to give us a heads-up, and advanced notice of who's at our door. Rhoda had none of those advantages. Perhaps she simply asked, "Who is it?" Whatever happened at that door, we do know that, though she didn't see him, she recognized his voice.

Now, let's go over that again. She:

- prayed for him (Vv. 5 & 12),
- heard the knock (v. 13),
- rose from praying to answer the door (v. 14),
- ran to tell the others the good news (v. 14), and
- left the door closed and locked (v. 14).

While reading this scripture did you ever ask, "Gee, why didn't she open the door?" After reading this chapter several times over the years, it dawned on me to ask that question. Whenever you read the Bible, and suddenly something grabs your attention, know that God is trying to tell you something. What was God going to reveal to me? What is He now going to reveal to you?

THE KNOCK

Acts 12:14 (NIV) says, "When she recognized Peter's voice, she was so overjoyed she ran back without opening it and exclaimed, 'Peter is at the door!'" How much greater her joy could've been if she had opened the door and been the first to welcome him inside.

Did she want to kick herself, question herself later or have a "Duh!" moment? What about you? Did you ever experience anything like this? I certainly have. I've listened to many Rhoda stories as people were honestly testifying (versus *testilying*).

It is written in James 1:22(AMP), *"But prove yourselves doers of the word [actively and continually obeying God's precepts], and not merely listeners [who hear the word but fail to internalize its meaning], deluding yourselves [by unsound reasoning contrary to the truth]."* Ouch! What was Rhoda supposed to do when she heard the knock? Open the door! When we *ask, seek and knock*, we want God to make haste and respond to us. Shouldn't He expect the same of us? Why has it taken me so long to get this? Please, let me help you.

In the Gospel of John, chapter 18:16, Peter was standing on the outside of a door as Jesus was being interrogated inside. John gained permission to let him in. Rhoda didn't seem to need to get permission to let Peter in.

Rhoda, Open Up!

Some of you may remember the game Atari. It's creator, Nolan Bushnell, once stated, "Everyone who's ever taken a shower has had an idea. It's the person who gets out of the shower, dries off, and does something about it who makes a difference."[3] It doesn't matter if you hear the knock because you prayed, or just because God is speaking. If you recognize the voice to be God's, then it's time to get out of the shower, open the door and let Him in.

I made a decision to open the door to my heart. I want to be a doer of the word, fulfiller of the dream and conqueror of the quest God has laid out for me. It shall be done as long as He is in the lead.

I'm excited to see what lays ahead for me. Don't you want to see how to make your dreams a reality too? Come on; let me walk with you through the pages of this book so you can see where the end will bring you.

Things to consider:
Did you identify with anything in this chapter? What dreams, or ideas have you shared

THE KNOCK

with others, yet never fulfilled?
Knock, knock, knock!

Chapter 2

Praying for a Change

Then Jesus told his disciples a parable to show them that they should always pray and not give up.

Luke 18:1 (NIV)

Jesus taught the disciples the importance of persistent prayer. Whatever the circumstances are, most often it's going to take more than a microwave prayer to get results. We always want instant results but seldom get it. It does happen, just not often. There've been times while the words were still on my lips, the phone rang, and I had my request granted. Those times are very few and very far apart.

However, when I'm behind on my credit card payments (Lord, forgive me) and there's a conference or event I really need to attend, I spend the day and night in prayer asking which way I should go. I hate getting notified about past due bills. Don't they know I have a conference to go to? They've got to let me use the card one more time. This may not be a financial crisis to you, but it is to me. How would you handle it?

When I'm feeling empty or inadequate to serve, I'll stay in the house for days praying. Have you ever been there? It's quite possible that one of you is there right now. It seems like you're not progressing in the faith. Where's the fruit?

Do you ever wonder what Jesus was going through when He would go out early in the morning to pray? What did He say to His Father? He wasn't praying about past due bills. He wasn't asking for a wife, promotion on the job, or new home. Was He just longing to communicate and fellowship with God? Perhaps He just needed to gain strength to stay heavenly minded.

There're times I just want to get closer to Jesus. I want to touch Him; feel His heartbeat. That's when you stay on your knees until you fall asleep. I find myself crying out, "Lord, I need to go up on the mountain." Have your prayers ever been done by groaning or moaning because you didn't have the words? Thank God we can depend on the Holy Spirit - "In the same way, the Spirit helps us in our weakness. We do not know what we ought to pray for, but the Spirit himself intercedes for us with groans that words cannot express. And he who searches our hearts knows the mind of the Spirit, because the Spirit intercedes for the saints in accordance with God's will." (Romans 8:26, 27 NIV)

Did Rhoda pray like that? She wasn't a well-educated person. It's likely none of them were, surely not Peter. She didn't have a book on how to intercede when your friend is in jail, no Bible or concordance to make sure she used the right words; she just cried out from her heart.

There are times when God will call you to get away to spend time with Him. There are times when He may want you to make some permanent adjustments to get away from friends, family, workplaces, etc. I love to spend time alone. I think my friends, who have told me that I need to get out more, would've used the words of Rufus M. Jones to describe me. He wrote, referring to saints, canonized and not, "These persons live by inward insight instead of argument; experience of God instead of speculation about Him. It must be said at once that the saint is not, like the poet, born that way."[1]

I've been told I was, "ahead of my time" or "born out of time." I'm not positive what they meant, but I do know it was said in reference to the time I spent in communion with God. My thought processes and conversations seemed to show that I had spent time in His word and in His presence. That was the greatest season of my life. (I'll discuss that in detail in a future book.)

Another saying that I've heard in reference to my "alone" time is, "Don't be so heavenly bound that you're no earthly good." I believe the only way to be any earthly good is to keep your mind on Jesus: be heavenly bound. Colossians 3:2 admonishes us to, "Set your mind on things above, not on things on the earth."

Though I enjoyed being alone, that's not always the same as separating myself to be with Him. Have you ever done like Elijah or Jonah and tried to separate yourself by running away from God?

Other times, when my friends weren't really loving on me, they'd accuse me of being antisocial. What made me do some serious soul searching was reading Proverbs 18:1, "A man who isolates himself seeks his own desire; He rages against all wise judgment." Ooh, that sounds ugly. I did say at the beginning that God sometimes speaks to us through others. However, if we isolate ourselves, we may miss some good counsel from those who can guide us in various areas. Someone might even give you an opportunity to use the gifts God gave you so you can bear fruit. I've applied a little effort and have increased my social activities. This made it necessary to learn social graces. The tendency to share my thoughts makes me appear, to some, to be opinionated. Humph! Another term that was used to describe me was *brutally honest*. This was said of me over twenty years ago. The hurt I felt was deep, and it was years before I realized that was a reflection of my upbringing. My mother never bit her tongue or curtailed her angst when speaking to my siblings and me. It's never my intent to be brutal, only honest. Don't you appreciate that? Please say, yes. Recently I was told that I speak and write with clarity. I've come a long way. Thank You, Jesus.

What about Rhoda? Do you think she'd been in the house too long, not enough socializing? Was she so excited to have the group all there with her that she just wanted to feel included? Sharing this experience of having heard Peter's voice could have made her feel like she had a greater purpose. Was it just the joy of knowing that their prayers were answered that sent her running off to tell the others without opening the door?

Matthew Henry comments that as long as we are kept waiting for a mercy, we must continue praying for it. However, "sometimes that which we most earnestly wish for, we are most backward to believe...."[2]

Paul gives us an exhortation, in 1 Thessalonians 5:17, to "pray without ceasing." God is still in the prayer answering business. Yet, too often, we can't seem to grab and hold on to the answer. We won't get the manifestations of the answers that are within our reach if we don't:

- recognize it's the answer (James 1:5),
- understand the will of God (Ephesians 5:17),
- make haste (Psalm 119:60), and
- let go of fear (Psalm 34:4).

Why haven't you opened the door? Each of the above items has a scripture in parenthesis. Read them. When you've done that, read the following illustrations.

Recognizing the answer

We had the second worst snowstorm in New

Jersey history on the weekend of January 23-24, 2016. One of the ministers had a conference call worship service. During testimony time, a young lady said she had been out of work for months. In His loving kindness, God gave wisdom to someone in a position of authority at a corporation. That person created a new position in the company, and this young lady was hired to fill it. It wasn't her field of expertise, nor did it pay what she wanted. She did recognize God was doing something great for her, so she accepted the position. I'm waiting with excitement to hear her follow-up testimony.

Let's say you've been praying for a career where God will use your engineering degree. You get a call from a professional job hunter who offers you a position in the accounting department of a well-known firm. You rationalize that since your degree is in engineering, this can't possibly be the job for you. Besides, you've never worked in accounting and don't believe the salary offered will support your desired lifestyle.

Let me see, you've been praying for a position where God can use your qualifications; your unemployment checks have run out; the mortgage is due, now the cable is off, but this isn't what you were looking for. You feel comfortable working with numbers if you're working in a computer lab; yet, you can't recognize the connection to work in a financial type of lab. God knows what you can do better than you do. ~~Those~~ *your* abilities and knowledge ~~you've gained~~ to work with numbers came from God.

Don't suffer from tunnel vision. I've been told to "step out of the box." (I've also been told to stay in my own lane. I'll get to that in another chapter.) How can we say we have faith, then say, "I can't do that"? Just because you haven't tried it before doesn't mean you can't. Why don't you confess, Philippians 4:13, "I can do all things through Christ who strengthens me."?

Ask God for wisdom; don't just dismiss a new idea. You may start with less salary than you wanted, but by simply excelling in the new position, or networking with others in this corporation, you may get opportunities to exceed your financial desires.

Understand the will of God

I heard this story on the radio several months after hurricane Katrina. It was from a lady who had lived in New Orleans. She was sure God told her to move to Atlanta; that's where she would find the employment she was looking for. She wondered how she could uproot her family and move. She was active in her church and settled into her ascribed status. She had good and bad anxiety over the prospect of moving, yet, still hadn't made any arrangements to do so. She was asked, "Didn't you trust God to take care of you in Atlanta?" She said she did and sought advice. She was advised to follow the normal steps. This would have included sending out resumes, applying for apartments and getting references from her pastor for a new church home. She didn't budge, indeed, lacking the audacity to follow through. Fear made her believe she would be stuck in New Orleans, doomed to poverty as her family had been for generations.

Well, a storm arose. Through the subsequent events of Hurricane Katrina, she ended up in Atlanta. How much better her transition could have been if she hadn't delayed. Not only would she and her children have avoided that tragedy, but also perhaps she would've been well enough established to send for her family to join her.

Does it need to take a storm for you to open up the door and allow God to step in and take over?

Make Haste

"I just prayed about this last night and wasn't expecting an answer so soon." Have you ever said that? How about, *"I need more time to make sure that's what I really want."* God knows as we're praying if we are playing with ideas or are really ready to commit to a change. Nevertheless, sometimes He'll put us to the test.

It's happened to me. I wanted to further my education, so prayed about returning to school. My daughter and her husband, who were living with me, at the time, had recently moved to Florida. The apartment was too large for my needs. The apartment had six and a half large rooms with an attic. I didn't want to be alone in that much space. On top of that, the first floor had been vacant for several months. Neither did I have the time or money to maintain it. I prayed and offered to give it all up if God could just find a room for me to live in. Then I'd use the extra money and energy to go back to school.

The very next day, someone I barely knew asked me if I'd be interested in taking over her apartment so she could go to North Carolina to school. She didn't want to leave her place empty or give it up. What?! I answered, yes, before taking the time to ask myself if I was crazy. Later I found out she felt the same way. She couldn't believe she asked me, pretty much a stranger, to move into her place, her space with all her belongings.

I met her through a co-worker two or three years prior. We had run into each other at church services a few times, and once three of us went to dinner together. We had kindred spirits and she was on my prayer list. I found myself being led to pray for her often, and even to call her "pastor" as I did. She wasn't a pastor, and when I ran into her one day, I told her about that. She very sarcastically replied, "What's that supposed to be, a prophecy?" I was a little put off by that, yet, I continued to pray for her as I was led. Now, a little over a year later and already she was packing to go to seminary for a Master of Divinity degree. (It was a prophecy after all.) On the other hand, I hadn't even applied to any schools yet.

I had never been to her apartment, as I said our time together over that period was minimal. I started wondering if I had made a mistake. She actually had two connecting apartments. One she used to live in, the other as her office and storage space. Now, I had six very large rooms to take care of again. I was blessed because I no longer had to pay utilities, and she had laundry facilities. I saved a great deal on the rent also. I set up most of my furniture in the office space. I had to rearrange her living and dining room area to add my sofa and end tables. (That's how large the area was.) We were both expecting great changes. God answered both of our prayers. She was ready, but I wasn't.

She went to seminary for three years and graduated with honors. She's said on several occasions she wouldn't have left her apartment to go so far away if I hadn't agreed to these arrangements. She would have because she was following God. Providence would have prevailed.

I stated some of my benefits for this suddenly answered prayer. I prayed for years that God would make a way for me to further my education. I thought I needed a degree in spite of hearing Him say, "I will teach you everything you need to know."

Thank You very much, but I want to go to college. God had a plan, but I didn't have a clue.

I had a passion for knowledge since grammar school. Life issues kept interrupting me in one way or another from continuing my education. A few years after high school I did complete a course to become a lab technician and worked in a chemical lab. A year later, it closed up for good. At about the same time laboratories began requiring a college degree. That was the end of that.

I had paid so many registration fees to various colleges they should have owed me, at least, one year of classes. Each time I went forward, a setback stopped me before starting. Twice, I had to have major surgery just before the semesters began. I was so discouraged that I finally gave up. However, in His merciful, lovingkindness God opened up a way for me to start classes at Nyack, Manhattan Center just before I moved into this sister's apartment. I was so elated. I did it; I did it, and I was beside myself. Now, both of us would have our hearts desires fulfilled.

Nope! The attacks on the World Trade Center shut down my dream. September 11, 2001, aside from the obvious casualties, caused the death and destruction of many survivors' dreams. I'm not being selfish when I think of how it affected my life. My eyes swell with tears whenever I think about it.

The year after 9/11, I resigned from my

employment of almost twenty-two years. I had wrestled with doing so for at least five years' prior and was convinced it was the right thing to do. I didn't have the courage or, financial security necessary, nor a degree to find another prosperous position. I was hoping God would again move <u>suddenly</u>, in response to my prayers. He didn't.

I was miserable and suffering from claustrophobia, more so after 9/11. The location I worked in changed and the environment was suffocating me. The windows had wired screens; my workstation was small and had high walls to discourage conversation with co-workers. I felt chained to my desk by the headset and wanted to escape. I sought counsel and explained why it was necessary to resign. Someone reminded me what the Bible says in 2 Thessalonians 3:10, if you don't work, you don't eat. Finally, I got the courage and wrote a letter of resignation. It was the most liberating day of my life. No, the second, meeting Jesus gave me the most liberation.

This time, I made haste, not God. I was unemployed for almost two years. God used that time to teach me some very precious lessons. The first was that He would provide for me, in spite of my foolishness. He magnified His word above His name and supplied all of my need. I didn't have to beg for bread either.[3] I requested monies from an Income Security Plan the company offered to cover particular circumstances. This plan was established to provide for employees if a layoff occurred or a location closed and would cause inconvenience to travel to another office. Well, the office I worked in before being transferred to Manhattan had closed. They initially refused to approve it for me. However, God stepped in and worked it out for my good.

Let go of fear

Let's visit the example of the engineer again.

"I followed my father into engineering; that must be the career for me. He would be so disappointed if I changed paths." It's always better to follow God. You might be qualified for one thing, but it still may not be where God wants you.

Hebrews 13:8(Amp) says, "Jesus Christ (the Messiah) is (always) the same, yesterday, today (yes), and forever (to the ages)." He never said that about us. There's also a verse of a song we sing in church that says, "The world is ever changing, but You are still the same...."[4] Yes, the world is ever-changing; the word of God stays the same. However, we need to change. We either:

- don't ever see a need to change – that may be foolish,
- see the need to change, but won't – that's rebelliousness,
- see the need but don't know how to change – now you're approaching wisdom.

Fear can keep you from progressing, prospering, and changing. Anxiety comes with any kind of change. Don't give up. Get up and over it.

When praying for a change, it's most important to get to the place where you open the door to your hearts. Haven't you heard this before: PUSH - <u>p</u>ray <u>u</u>ntil <u>s</u>omething <u>h</u>appens. Progress will be realized if you listen to the voice of God and follow the instructions He gives. All of them. If God says do A, B, C and D and you do A, B, and D, you've been disobedient. Change only comes when you are committed and submitted to the will of God. He doesn't care how excited any of us are about hearing from Him. He won't care how many people we tell our story to unless we have a true testimony to confirm that we heard His voice, and responded by opening the doors of our hearts, being obedient to His instructions. A. W. Tozer said, *"Truth will not give itself to a rebel."*[5] The truth is revealed in obedience. Obedience comes from letting the truth into our hearts and living it out. Being inspired isn't good enough. The real joy comes from trusting and obeying.

There were three topics of interest to me in Lyndon B. Johnson's inaugural address. They were titled *Justice and Change, Liberty and Change*, and the third was, *Union and Change.* However, it was difficult for him to make the change from the Senate to the Presidency. He wanted it, positioned himself for it, then backed down. The 1960 nomination went to John F. Kennedy instead. Johnson was groomed for the role but stopped short of pursuing his dream for no apparent reason. According to biographer Robert A. Caro, fear stopped him even though he had declared from his youth that he would be president.[6]

Sometimes, God has a plan *B*. He had a plan *B* for Abraham, Moses, and a host of others too numerous to name. Fate stepped in for Johnson, and he later became the president.

A folder titled *"Good Intentions"* has filled up the file cabinet of our lives. We had one or more dreams we intended to pursue, but... someone said good intentions are the same as disobedience. I like to call them dressed up lies, excuses for not doing what we know we should.

His sheep know His voice and follow Him. Open the door; you know it's God! Open up in faith or open up in fear, but open the door to your heart, let Him in and follow Him. There is something awesome waiting for you on the other side. Don't let someone else take the promotion, the bonus, the opportunity or anything else that God has for you. Oh, sure you've heard it said many times, "What God has for me is for me." Well, listen, I've seen God move His operation right along without me. Have you ever been told that God doesn't need you? Yes, He has great plans to prosper you, but you have to follow His voice.

"You warned them in order to turn them back to your law, ... 'The person who obeys them will live by them.'" (Nehemiah 9:29 NIV) Even, when what you hear isn't a warning, you need to do more than be filled with joy because you heard from God. You have to let Him in to do whatever He wants to in order to receive His best for your life.

Let me share one more personal testimony concerning this. Again, it refers to my struggle to make a career change. My eagerness to make a change didn't begin in 2001; it intensified around this time.

I had been working for a large nationwide corporation for fifteen years at this point. I began in, what was then called, the customer service department. It was great; I enjoyed helping people solve problems. I never liked sales, but it was a part of my required duties. As the company evolved (I should say mutated), my title changed to "sales representative." As long as I could improve my client's service and find solutions to their problems, I was still able to sell.

Rhoda, Open Up!

Eventually, corporate greed became the new norm. I found myself in a high-pressured sales department, and I hated it. Service was almost eliminated. I now loathed going to work each day. There wasn't any satisfaction in trying to force products down people's throats, especially when they were calling because of a problem. I understood the dynamics of competition and profits, but there really should have been a cutoff point. Each month we were given new goals to reach. Some of my co-workers, out of fear, were padding customer accounts trying to reach their goals. People were paying for products they didn't even know they had.

One night, I had a dream. I was looking out of my office window when I saw a giant of a man, dressed in a business suit, holding a blimp as though it were a bat. He came nearer and hit the side of the building. I yelled for everyone to run and get out of the building. It looked as though he was going to swing the blimp again. People started running down the stairs and out onto the street. When I got to the ground floor, I ran into a stall in the bathroom and sat on the toilet. When I awoke, I tried to analyze my dream. I understood that the toilet represented elimination. I wondered why I didn't leave the building like everyone else.

The dream and my growing distaste with my work requirements filled my mind with thoughts of leaving. In spite of myself, God blessed me to excel in sales. However, I constantly felt guilty because I would praise God for the increase in bonuses, then cry out for Him to open a way for me to get out of there. I put in transfers to other departments but got nowhere. Others were being transferred, but I was left there getting more and more depressed.

Finally, I was promoted and sent to work in another city. I thought that was the answer to my prayers. It proved to be a short-term opportunity and more stressful than I could have imagined. There were ten of us squeezed into a small room. Our desks were connected and lined up so close to the walls we had to scoot in if anyone wanted to pass by. We didn't get paid overtime because we were management. The only thing this promotion did was add fuel cost, commute time and aggravation.

The following year it was announced the office would be moving much farther away from where I lived or was willing to drive each day. I requested a downgrade and went back to my old position. Don't let anyone make you feel ashamed to go back. Going back doesn't always mean going backward.

I made major contributions to that corporation when I went back. I also got to see many of my ideas implemented throughout the company. The fact that I never received acknowledgment above the local level was not a motivation to leave. I just knew that I had to get out of there. I wasn't willing to quit. Where was I going? I had great benefits and was getting a very good salary. I felt paralyzed.

I needed to hear from God. He was speaking, knocking at my heart, but I hadn't answered. I became sensitive to Scriptures such as:

- Joshua 1:9 "Have I not commanded you? Be strong and of good courage; do not be afraid, nor be dismayed, for the LORD your God *is* with you wherever you go."
- Proverbs 3:5 "Trust in the Lord with all your heart and lean not on your own understanding."
- Isaiah 41:10 "Fear not, for I *am* with you; Be not dismayed, for I *am* your God. I will strengthen you, Yes, I will help you, I will uphold you with My righteous right hand."

That's how I made it through that time. Often, these words would comfort me. Sometimes, I would hear these scriptures on Christian radio, in a sermon, or from strangers who crossed my path. It was encouraging, for a little while, to know that God was aware of my pain. I let these words into my heart and held onto them for dear life.

Still, after September 11, it seemed like every part of my life had a breakdown. After a while, I didn't want to hear those verses anymore. In my mind, I had let them in; now, I wanted them to leave. There wasn't any reason I could find to suffer anymore, so, I left. It took three years to recover from my *self-inflicted wounds*. Change, I learned, must be orchestrated by God.

Self-inflicted wounds are what you bear when you do things your way. They can come as financial loss, spiritual constipation, depression, and low self-worth. Take Moses for instance. He knew he would one day be the deliverer of his people. However, when he tried to do it his way, he ended up on a mountain with sheep and goats. God sat him aside for a while, a long while.

Imagine, if you can, this conversation between Moses and God.

Moses: You called me to be a deliverer. I studied hard; learned history, several languages, and am good at management. Now, I'm eighty years old, and all I can do is tend to sheep? I'll never be anything but a failure.

God: I called you before you were born. I predestined you to lead My people out of Egypt, but you didn't wait for the knock. Can you hear me now? Do you see that burning bush?

When He did call Moses to go forth, all of his confidence had faded. This was because of his "*self-inflicted*" wound.[7]

It's written in Romans 12:2 that we are to be *transformed*. How, you ask? By the renewing of our minds. Transformed means changed. God expects us to change our way of thinking. This will reflect changes in many areas of our lives. We forgive when our minds have been transformed. We share, we love, we care, we stop doing the things God hates and begin doing what we know will please Him.

Jesus' coming reflected all kinds of changes. The religious system went through a mighty transformation. The veil of the temple was torn. Now, we all have access to God, through the Savior. Jews and Gentiles can come together before the throne of grace with boldness.

He gave us His word, and His Holy Spirit to help enable us to change. We have everything we need to live in a godly manner. What more can we ask for? We may ask for more grace, and yes, praise God, He gives us that too.

It's written in Malachi 3:6, *"For I am the Lord, I do not change; that is why you, O sons of Jacob, are not consumed."* Matthew Henry's commentary says, "The people of Israel had reason to say that he was an unchangeable God, for he had been faithful to his covenant with them and their fathers. They had been false and fickle in their conduct to him, and he might justly have abandoned them; but because he remembered his covenant, they were preserved."[8]

He will keep His promise to rapture us and bring us home. He will change these vile bodies and give us a new outfit and a new name. We need to listen when He knocks and open the door to welcome Him in. *"I correct and punish everyone I love. So make up your minds to turn away from your sins. Listen! I am standing and knocking at your door. If you hear my voice and open the door, I will come in and we will eat together"* (Revelation 3:20 CEV).

By the way, I found work in the customer service field. I would never have considered working as a home health care aide, but that's what I ended up doing. I loved taking care of people and helping enhance their living experience. One of my earliest cases was to fill-in for another aide who was going on vacation. The daughter met with me and explained that her mother was blind and spoke French and only a little English. She assured me if I followed her instructions that I would be able to handle it. When we went into her mother's room, she said a few words in French. I assumed she was telling her why I was there. Her mother replied to her, and she translated what she said. This blind woman told her she would be fine with me because she could tell I was a Christian. That was after being in her home about thirty minutes, and in her presence about two minutes.

After that experience, it was easy for me to use this position to minister to people whom I could never have reached while sitting behind a desk. I found that I have the gifts of helps and service. I had gotten so used to talking to people in a disembodied way (over the phone), that it was difficult to express myself in person. When others feared public speaking, I found it easier to stand behind a pulpit and speak. It took a while to learn to talk to people face-to-face again. I could have sown many more seeds, and bore much more fruit if my timing had

Praying for a Change

been better. I worked in the field for five years before being promoted to Medical Coordinator. God had been faithful to supply my every need in spite of the fluctuation in salary sometimes from week-to-week. This promotion brought consistency to my income and financial increase. My final position there was as the compliance coordinator. God is great!

I didn't correctly interpret that earlier dream about "elimination." I believe that's when I should have left the company I hated so much. The direction for me to take wasn't clear. Doubt and fear hindered by ability to trust God and be led out. (That building is empty now. Some of my co-workers were laid off, some transferred to other departments, but everyone had to leave that location.)

Has God been calling you to make some kind of change in your life, something you never dreamed of? Are you afraid to step out of the box?

God told the Israelites that they were to stay camped as long as the cloud was over the tabernacle. When the cloud moved, they were to move.[9] For some of you, the cloud has moved, but you're still camped in the same place you've been for years. When God moves the cloud, follow it.

It's urgent that you continue reading because there's an awesome young man who shares what God has done in his life. You don't want to miss it.

Don't you hear Him knocking? Don't you recognize His voice? Won't you trust Him? What dreams, or desires have you believed came from God, yet, are still waiting to be realized? Don't you want to look back over your life a year from now and see how you've overcome obstacles that prevented you from being "more than a conqueror?"

Things to consider:

Did you find a reason to answer the questions you found in this chapter? Are you stuck in a rut at work or church? Have you sought the will of God in those areas of your life? How many times have you shared that information with others? Did you follow through with the instructions God gave you? Are you ready to do so now?

Hush, I hear a sound.

Knock, knock, knock.

Chapter 3

The First Responders

Take fast hold of instruction; let her not go; for she is thy life.

Proverbs 4:13(KJV)

Rhoda, Open Up!

In the last chapter, I talked about plan "*B*". Don't ignore the knocking depending on getting a second chance; it may not come. It's always better to let God into your situation immediately. Taking fast hold of instructions will give you a better reward. If you don't appreciate the value of hearing the *Voice* or grab a hold of that doorknob right away and let Him in someone else may step up to the plate, and like Jacob did to Esau, take your blessing.

There are those who, as in Rhoda's story, were the first to respond to what she heard. Those are the "*Yea, hath God said*"[1] folks or naysayers. Rhoda didn't have any doubt that it was Peter. She wasn't concerned about being deceived, she was absolutely certain. Nevertheless, the others, as too often happens, responded by trying to convince her that she was wrong. Like the serpent in the Garden of Eden, they tried to put doubt in her mind. Those who were with Rhoda said, "Thou art mad." The names of these people aren't listed. The scripture just says, "the church" had gathered at the house to pray. We do know, according to Acts 12:12, they were at Mary's house, the mother of John Mark. Was he there? Were any of the Apostles there? It certainly is likely they were. This was the usual gathering place; Peter's going there assures us of this. So, we have the elders of the church, these Holy Spirit-filled leaders, plus the lay folk all gathered together fervently praying. One lowly servant girl tells them their prayers have been answered. She kept insisting and wouldn't be dissuaded. They were equally persistent that this couldn't be Peter himself at the door. So, they tried to silence her by saying it was his angel. If they believed that, they were assuming he was now dead.

When we hear from God, we often speak to our leaders for confirmation. Sometimes, they, like those around Rhoda, tell us "Thou art mad." They may try to shake your faith and have you believe, as Joseph's brothers tried to do, that what you heard is too grand for you. If you persist, they may envy you as Joseph's brothers envied him. I heard a bishop recall an incident when his faithful, Holy Spirit-filled, co-laborer tried to dissuade him from following the vision God gave him. He wanted to build a bigger church. He was told something comparable to, "Thou art mad." He was grieved at the lack of support; yet, he followed the Lord and had great success.

It's always good to seek counsel, but if you know, without a shadow of a doubt, that you've heard from God, then open the door, take that leap and follow your dream up with action. *"Take fast hold of instructions let her not go; for she is thy life."*

Take a moment to look briefly back over your life and remember the times you didn't pursue a dream because you couldn't find the encouragement you sought. Take only a moment; don't dwell on the past. This exercise is to prevent you from future regret. How many, "If only I had followed the *Voice*," thoughts did you come up with? How many times were you filled with joy because you discerned the Voice, told someone about it, but never opened the door to your heart to follow the instructions you were given? If only I had a dime for each time...

So many people experience regrets because when opportunity knocks, they don't answer. This reminds me of what I said earlier (Chapter 2) about changing lanes. Sometimes, that is exactly what needs to happen. Just because you've been an usher since you were ten years old, shouldn't mean you can't sing in the choir, (if you have the talent to do so).

You've been a nurse for fourteen years and now want to become a dietician. Go for it. If the management tries to downplay your choice for a career change or suggests you stay in your lane, look for another place to work where you can follow your heart. If we would just let God direct our path, we'd find ourselves crossing into lanes, and adding value to other areas of life and being fruitful more times than not. A dear friend gave an illustration one morning using a chicken potpie and a TV dinner. He talked about opening a TV dinner and finding that a few peas had slipped into the section with the mashed potatoes. Some people couldn't eat until they put those peas back where they belong. (How dare they change lanes?) However, a chicken potpie has peas in the mix, and everything together is delicious. The challenge is to evaluate your workplace, social life and even the church you affiliate yourself with and see if they're like potpies or TV dinners. If you find yourself pigeonholed into one role and are ready to follow God, rather than man, take a leap of faith and change lanes. Inaction comes from fear. Move! Any action is better than no action at all. You're blessed when you believe. That step forward is proof that you do. There will be a performance of those things that the Lord told you. Don't delay because of someone else's opinion.

What do you think would have happened if Noah had followed his peers instead of God? King David was a shepherd, the runt of the family. But God called him to be a king. Gideon, is another example. He went from threshing wheat, to become a military leader. It's likely that even his father wouldn't have called him to lead an army against the Midianites. Don't forget about Ruth. She left her family and all that she was familiar with to go to another country. I believe she was led by God to follow her mother-in-law, Naomi. She's listed in the genealogy of Christ. Finally, Paul, who caused the death of many Christians, then became the most recognized religious leader of his day. Which one of them would have gotten approval from their peers or leaders? All of these people heard from God, changed lanes, and are known throughout the world.

STOP! **S**top, **t**hink, **o**bserve and **p**ray before you go running off on a wild tangent. Think things through; observe the situation your revelation presented to you. Pray for confirmation before proceeding. God will continue to prepare you for the task He's set before you if your heart is right. He may need to teach you to disagree without being disagreeable or to respect those who have charge over you. When you're sure, as Rhoda was, of whose voice you've heard, then open that door, let Him in and go for it! Allow the God of hope to fill you with all joy and peace in believing.

Whenever we apply the words of God to our lives, it will build faith. There is life in *them-there-words*. The word of God is alive and speaking to us still. *He* is speaking to you now. When you open the door of your heart and receive the word by faith, it will give you courage, peace, wisdom and joy. Of course, there are times you may have to suffer a little while because of the critic's reactions. Nevertheless, have faith in God. Don't let anyone turn you around.

While you're trying to convince them of what was revealed to you, that knocking might stop. Then what will you be left with, aside from regret? It doesn't matter if you receive revelation through Bible study, a message you heard in church, the radio, TV ministry, or even through social media, God will watch over His word to perform it. It won't return to Him void. Practice listening to His voice and be ready when He speaks.

Another dear friend of mine shared with me her regrets for refusing to act on what she was told. She was making good money and had the gift of giving. She was constantly praying for wisdom in managing her finances. She got a call one evening from her pastor's wife who made arrangements to meet her at the diner. Over dinner, she told her God had put it on her heart to share a lesson on financial management. She even took out paper and pen to write and draw a table to make sure she understood. She was so excited and went home and told her family about the blessing. She couldn't believe this woman of God had met with her. She was awed that God had answered her prayers. She made a few adjustments but never applied all of the instructions and in a short time, reverted back to her bad habits. Now, twenty years later, she regrets her disobedience. She didn't take fast hold of the instructions.

God has blessed us with beautiful sun-shining

days, star-bright nights, flowers and birds, and so much more to entertain us. He isn't entertaining us with suggestions, neither tickling our ears. He's speaking to His children and it's urgent to respond in faith. We are to "try the spirits"; for we know our adversary delights in lying to us. He will steal, kill and destroy our hopes, dreams, self-esteem and very life if we let him. Then he'll mock us by telling us how foolish we were. He'll give us all the help he can to keep us under the burden of regret. There's nothing wrong with taking your situation to a mature saint to pray with you or counsel you. Pray and ask God who that, or they, should be. Just don't run off telling your friends that God spoke to you. When you start complaining again they'll remind you what *you* said God told you. Ask yourself: Why would they want you to pray for or counsel them with your poor record of letting God into your heart? If you're always telling people how good God is in answering your prayers, but your life is a wreck because of disobedience, they might doubt your testimony. *"You, then, who teach others, do you not teach yourself?"* (Romans 2:21 NIV). We say we trust God, but our actions/inactions say that we don't.

Does it ever seem like God is giving you the silent treatment? I've done that to my children. There have been times when I've asked, "Didn't I tell you before?" or "Why are you asking me that same question again?" It seemed like they weren't listening to me, so I'd give them the silent treatment for a period of time. There have been times when it hurt to watch them handle their *stuff*. It must really hurt God to see us doing the same when we've been so hardheaded and stubborn. However, it's amazing how often my children would remember the instructions I gave and use them, and all was well. If they didn't I would eventually get back to them. It is written in Mark 4:23-25 (AMP)

> 23 If anyone has ears to hear, let him hear *and* heed My words." Then He said to them, "Pay attention to what you hear. By your own standard of measurement [that is, to the extent that you study spiritual truth and apply godly wisdom] it will be measured to you [and you will be given even greater ability to respond]—and more will be given to you besides. For whoever has [a teachable heart], to him *more* [understanding] will be given; and whoever does not have [a yearning for truth], even what he has will be taken away from him."

This means that God sees I'm not responding to His voice, not opening the door to my heart, so why keep knocking? Hence, the silent treatment. This doesn't mean that He doesn't care, or has given up on us. No, He's waiting for us to seek Him with a heart bent toward obedience. Ask yourselves if you're waiting or procrastinating.

According to Webster's New World College Dictionary part of the definition for *wait* is:
1. to stay in a place or remain in readiness or in anticipation (until something expected happens or for someone to arrive or catch up),
2. to be ready or at hand [dinner was waiting for them], or
3. to remain temporarily undone or neglected [let that job wait]

However, according to Strong's Concordance, the word "*wait*" used in Psalm 27:14 means:
1. to bind together (perhaps by twisting), i.e. collect; (figuratively) and
2. to expect: gather (together), look, patiently, tarry, wait (for, on, upon)

When we truly wait for God to answer our prayers, we should draw near to Him with periods of quiet meditation. We should thank Him in advance for His consideration of our request, then worship and adore Him. Waiting should be a time of preparation, not procrastination.

If you are waiting for a promotion, you may need to use the time to take a course or update your credentials. See if the company you work for offers classes for additional training. Whatever you need to do, do it! Prepare while you wait.

If you're waiting to purchase a house, check

your credit report, see how much of a mortgage you can get. Go to seminars and learn about homeowner associations (HOA) before you get tripped up in one.

If you're waiting for a spouse, ask a person you really trust to do an assessment of you. Then work on making the recommended adjustments.

You say you want to enjoy life more, yet, you never want to do anything or go anywhere. Perhaps you need to adjust your diet or take vitamins to increase your energy. Start by getting a physical. Remember what God said about those who always want to be alone. (Read Proverbs 18:1 again.) Get out and about! Don't waste a lot of time waiting for someone to join you. There are many things to do and places you can go alone and enjoy a great time.

When we wait by *binding/twisting* our threads of faith to His love and wisdom through prayer, we form a strong rope, which will draw us near to God. When the time is right, the Holy Spirit will speak, and an answer will be manifested. Hebrews 3:15 says: *while it is said, "Today if ye will hear His voice, do not harden your hearts as in the rebellion."*

"Procrastination" is from a Latin word meaning to *put off doing something until a future time, to postpone.*[2] This can refer to something unpleasant. Fear and stress can make almost anything seem unpleasant. Did you ever use the expression "procrastination is the thief of time"? You know who the real thief is, don't you? It's the devil, Satan.

When you vacillate between faith and fear bind your heart with God's and respond to His voice. Put your eyes on Jesus. He won't lead you astray.

One more scripture may help you understand how important it is to "take fast hold of instructions." In Revelation 2:21 (AMP) it is written, "I gave her time to repent [to change her inner self and her sinful way of thinking], but she has no desire to repent of her immorality *and* refuses to do so." Don't let the enemy of your soul deceive you into believing that you have plenty of time to obey. Don't let him convince you that tomorrow belongs to you; today may be the last day you'll hear the knock. Recognize the voice and take the opportunity to let Him in.

While it is still called *today* repent and prepare to march. Self-pity and regret are enemies to our souls.

Things to consider:

How are you using the time God has given you? Are you more intimate with God today than you were a year or two ago? Have you been waiting for *things* to change, or are you ready to be changed?

The First Responders

Knock, knock, knock.

Chapter 4

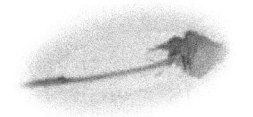

Appearances

When Jesus got up the next morning, he was hungry. He started out for the city, and along the way he saw a fig tree. But, when he came to it, he found only leaves and no figs. So he told the tree, "You will never again grow any fruit!" Right then the tree dried up.

Matthew 21:18-19 (CEV)

How many people do you know like the fig tree? Have you ever examined your spiritual life in the same manner you've examined others? Try it and make sure you use the same microscope. What do you see when you look *in* you?

First, let me share what my research on fig trees revealed. According to Nelson's Illustrated Encyclopedia of Bible Facts[1], the fruit of the fig tree appears before the leaves. These trees grow full without much height. When the leaves are of some size, small white flowers fill their interiors. If the leaves grow out without the figs having appeared yet, then the tree would stay barren throughout the season.

Now, look at yourself. Would your assessment be anything like this?

- I never miss Sunday service – Leaves.
- I even teach Sunday School - more leaves.
- I go to Bible Study - large leaves.
- I participate in a few ministries - larger leaves.
- I pay my tithes and give offerings - white flowers budding.
- I attend prayer services – Bingo! Lush with a lot of beautiful large leaves, spreading branches and lovely white flowers in abundance.

But where is the fruit?

The Greek word for this tree is *"syke."*[2] That's interesting. According to Webster's New World College Dictionary, the English word *"sycophant"* (sik'-a-fant), means:

> *Informer, lit., maker of the sign of the fig/ a person who seeks favor by flattering people of wealth or influence; parasite, toady.*

This may be conjecture, but what if the origin of the slang expression, *"psych"* is related to "syke." Its meaning is, *"to cause to be disturbed mentally or excited emotionally."* Can you see where I'm going with this? It may be hyperbole to say we *syke/psych* ourselves by thinking we're bearing fruit while we're only bearing beautiful leaves and barren trees. The leaves from the fig tree were big enough for Adam and Eve to use as a temporary covering when they were trying to hide from God in the Garden of Eden. Are you trying to use leaves as a covering? Do you say the right words, memorize the right verses, attend the right services just for appearance sake? Or are you a branch abiding in the vine? The litmus test is the fruit you bear. John 15:5 (NKJV) says, *"I am the vine, you are the branches; he who abides in Me and I in him, he bears much fruit, for apart from Me you can do nothing."* Much fruit, not much leaves!

What will Jesus say to you? Will He curse you as He did the fig tree? Will you be numbered with those as in John 15:6 *"If anyone does not abide in Me, he is cast out as a branch and is withered, and they gather them and throw them into the fire, and they are burned."*?

When you read this same story in the Gospel of Mark 11(Vv.11-30) the writer adds in verse 13, *"because it was not the season for figs."* Are you out of season? Did you get information from God about your purpose and then, like Moses, take matters into your own hands and fail? Well, be encouraged. The first part of John 15:2 says,*"Every branch in Me that does not bear fruit He takes away;"* There's a difference between that verse and John 15:6 because of the words *"abide in Me"* and *"not abide in Me."* I'm inclined to agree with Bruce Wilkinson whose research concluded that the term *"takes away,"* also means, *"take up."*[3] He explains that grape farmers have to lift up some vines and tie them to the trellis for them to bear fruit. I recently looked a little further into this and found and article online:

>*"Once the work of pruning is done, you want to lift up the cordons and gently secure them to your fence post, wire, or trellis using soft strips of cloth or garden ties. This allows the bearing vines to be up in the circulating breezes and bright sunshine where the developing clusters of fruit will sweeten to perfection."*[4]

It seems clear that John 15:2 is showing how

Appearances

God is trying to help those who abide in Him to bear more fruit.

Do you remember the story of Moses? He seemed to know that God would use him to bring the Israelites out of bondage. He didn't know how or when, so he used his own judgment. Wrong move! He went out one day and witnessed an Egyptian beating a Hebrew slave (Exodus 2:11-15). Moses decided this was his chance. So, he took matters into his own hands. After all, he wanted to help this oppressed slave, so he struck the Egyptian, and he died. Moses had many books at his disposal, but he didn't have the Bible. He hadn't read Habakkuk 2:3, *"For the vision is yet for an appointed time...though it tarry wait for it."* Life isn't like a card game, but can you imagine Kenny Rodgers singing, *"Know when to hold them. Know when to fold them. Know when to walk away. Know when to run"*? We need to know when to take fast hold of instructions, or tarry by listening to the Voice of God until clarity comes. Moses was banished to the mountain by his own guilt. In God's time, Moses brought forth fruit.

Do you realize the damage you can cause when you get ahead of God; when you are *out of season*? (*self-inflicted* wounds!) Oftentimes, we need to:

- Stand still and get to know God.
- Stand still and develop your fellowship with Him.
- Stand still and discern His voice.
- Stand still and wait on God's timing.
- Stand still until you understand His will.

You can't do anything, but make a mess, unless you abide in the True Vine. Learn the difference between waiting and procrastinating. (An excellent book to read that talks about the value of godly counsel and moving at the right time is *"Under Cover: The Promise of Protection Under His Authority,"* by John Bevere.)

We can cause damage under the guise of helping someone if the Spirit of God doesn't lead us in that way. It is mere pride to think that our good is God's good. I'm talking about things that aren't already specified in the Bible. You don't need to pray and wait for God to direct you in tithing or feeding the hungry. It's already written that we should. However, I've made mistakes ranging from loaning people money, without approval, to sharing my worldly wisdom. I was certain they would benefit from my experiences. My good ideas (or dare I say pride and self-righteousness), while instructing someone else how to handle their affairs turned out to be filthy rags. They lost a chance to reach out to God because I was in the way. I didn't bear fruit because I didn't ask for godly wisdom.

Unlike Rhoda, I had opened the door, but sin was crouching, and I let him in. Be careful and prayerful.

Stop eating from the wrong tree! Haven't you learned from what happened to Adam and Eve? Read this from Genesis 2:16-17:

> *"And the LORD God commanded the man, saying, "Of every tree of the garden you may freely eat; but of the tree of the knowledge of good and evil you shall not eat, for in the day that you eat of it you shall surely die."*

God gave Adam a few instructions:
- Be fruitful, multiply and fill the earth.
- Subdue it and have dominion over every living creature.
- Tend to the garden.
- Name the animals.

There was one thing God forbid Adam to do, <u>eat from the tree of knowledge</u>. Now that doesn't seem unreasonable to me. How about you? You do know what happened, don't you? The serpent lied to Eve. He convinced her God was hiding somethings from them. It didn't take the devil much to convince her that if they ate from the tree they would know as much as God; they would be like Him. Why do we still find ourselves eating from that tree?

How, do you ask? This is what we do whenever God knocks on the door of our hearts (or

Rhoda, Open Up!

our hard heads) with instructions. We take it to the *tree of the knowledge of good and evil* to question God. We evaluate what He said to determine if it's acceptable to us or not. Don't say you never do that. Many times, we weigh what we've heard (or read), with what we <u>think</u> we know. We heard the knock. We know the voice. Yet, we want to challenge God with our worldly wisdom. The enemy will find a way for us to ask ourselves, "Is God trying to keep something from us?", especially if we don't hear what we want to. We don't want Him to get over on us. It doesn't matter how excited we are to hear from Him.

We say we don't know what He means. Our lack of understanding the will of God isn't because He hasn't made Himself clear. It's because our thoughts have become so turbulent, so preoccupied with what we want, so undisciplined, that we can't focus on what we've heard. We're busy in our minds even when our bodies are sitting still or lying down. No rest, no peace.

It's all right to ask for understanding. The disciples had a hard time understanding Jesus while He was still with them.

- Matthew 15:17 – "Do you not yet understand..."
- Mark 8:17 – "Why do you reason... Do you not yet perceive nor understand?"
- Luke 9:45 – "But they did not

understand...and they were afraid to ask Him...."

They were afraid to ask Him! It's better to humbly ask Him for the grace to understand than to try to usurp His wisdom. When the knock is loud and clear, but you're not comfortable fulfilling His will, it won't matter how glad you are to hear from heaven: if you rebel, you are as guilty as Adam and Eve. We are often *not comfortable.*

"*Wisdom is the principal thing; therefore, get wisdom: and with all thy getting get understanding*" (Proverbs 4:7). We miss out on a lot of real good living when we waste time trying to debate with the Holy Spirit. Peter might have stayed outside for hours knocking, but I can assure you God won't. If you don't open the door of your heart and let Him in, your opportunity to grow will be put on hold. You may be put back on the shelf in the Carpenter's shop. Moses apparently lacked understanding and was on the shelf for forty years. The Potter's wheel isn't any fun either. He has plenty of clay that's waiting to be turned into a vessel of honor.

Things to consider:

Are you producing figs or flowers? Are you going through a period of pruning? If so, do you know why? Do you know what God is trying to accomplish in you? Has anyone noticed any positive changes in your life?

Knock, knock, knock! Is anyone home?

Chapter 5

Don't Tell – Go Show

Then Jesus said to him, "See that you don't tell anyone. But go, show yourself to the priest and offer the gift Moses commanded, as a testimony to them."

Matthew 8:4 (NIV)

Don't tell; go show. Oh, how we love to tell it all. We can be so quick to speak and once it's out there.... When we apply the word of God to our lives, we won't have to tell everyone what God said, the evidence will speak for itself. Wouldn't it be wonderful for someone to walk up to you and say, "I can see God is really working in your life; you've changed so much."? Have you ever told anyone you can see their spiritual growth? Wouldn't you like to hear that? Even if no one says these things, you'll know they see the change when they start asking you for advice or for you to pray for them or their family.

The evidence of a changed life lets the world know that you've opened the door of your heart and let Jesus in. This reminds me of the parable of the sower.

> *The sower sows the word [of God, the good news regarding the way of salvation]. These [in the first group] are the ones along the road where the word is sown; but when they hear, Satan immediately comes and takes away the word which has been sown in them. In a similar way, these [in the second group] are the ones on whom seed was sown on rocky ground, who, when they hear the word, immediately receive it with joy [but accept it only superficially];*
> Mark 4:14-16 (AMP).

The word sown on the stony ground was received, accepted and even welcomed at once with joy. Then what happens? Mark continues in verse 17:

> "*and they have no real root in themselves, so they endure only for a little while; then, when trouble or persecution comes because of the word, immediately they [are offended and displeased at being associated with Me and] stumble and fall away.*"

What happened is they felt good for a minute, but the word didn't do them any good because they didn't allow it to penetrate their hearts. This Scripture applies to salvation and I believe it applies anytime we don't let the Holy Spirit-filled word of God settle deep down within us.

I want to sing, what a wonderful change that has come over me. It'd be better if you were to sing that about me. Don't you want this to be your song?

The first time I surrendered to God, my co-workers kept asking me what was different about me. At first, it was difficult to explain. For years, I believed God was real, even that Jesus was His Son. As a matter-of-fact, I had read the Bible all the way through at least once by that time. I frequently attended church, even Sunday school. I made attempts to pray, but not in faith. I didn't understand what Jesus had done for me. I didn't believe He had done anything for me; yes, for others, but not for me. I didn't believe He could forgive or save me. I believed that He existed, and some people had a relationship with Him, but they were special. I had heard people give testimonies and wished He would do something for me. I can say that I didn't understand what I heard; I sure didn't have the faith to believe any of it would ever be applied to my life. If anything, I'd say I was jealous of the stories others shared about their walk with God. Sometimes, that made me sad, or angry. One day, I got it. I heard the Gospel preached in such a way that I could understand it and asked Jesus to be my Savior and Lord. I couldn't believe I had wasted so much time. It was so good to know that Jesus loved me too, cared for me, and was even willing and able to deliver me from so much guilt and shame. Yes, Jesus would provide everything I needed to live for Him, and He's given me so much more. I went through such a dramatic change that made it easy for others to know that something had happened, and they asked me about it. As I grow in the knowledge of Him, it's still awesome to have someone acknowledge that they can see my growth.

    I try to be mindful of my experience when I'm witnessing to people. I urge you to do the same. Try to remember the excitement you experienced and share that as you're telling someone about Jesus. No one wants to follow you to church or Jesus if you've lost the thrill of being His. Share the Gospel using scriptures, and your experiences. Too often, we'll bring someone to church and assume they comprehend what or whom the preacher is talking about. How can they know who David, Abraham or Paul were if they haven't been taught? Assume nothing! I was talking to a woman who had a parochial school education, yet, didn't have a clue who David was. At least twenty-five years had passed, and her children were now enrolled there. Yes, she called herself an A & P Christian. (For those who have never heard that expression it means Advent and Pentecost.) If she had ever heard of David, it's difficult to imagine forgetting him. Many people have heard, but don't understand terms such as salvation, redemption or justification. We have to spend the time needed to help them grasp these things and see their need to understand. Give them Jesus. Get them into a Bible study and take time asking and answering questions until you see a change in them. Make them feel like you care about them experiencing the benefits of salvation. They may be impressed with the dance ministry, or mass choir at your church for a minute, but it's the word of God that will save them. You want them to come into a knowledge of the truth. When they learn to meditate on the word of God and give themselves fully to Him, their profiting will appear to all. Then they too will know what it means, *don't tell; go show*. I don't want them just to get excited as Rhoda did. Is that all you want, a little excitement? We should be helping each other become mature Christians.

The Bible doesn't give any indication of what Rhoda's life was like before or after this scene. Just imagine if she hadn't told the others about Peter being at the door, and simply presented him when they walked back in the room together. Do you think her life would have been richer for it?

Let's go in another direction. Here's a story of a man who let the evidence speak for itself. He heard the call, responded in faith, opened the door, and let the Lord lead him into the great unknown. His name is Damon Jones or, as he prefers to be called, Damon "STEAM Teacher" Jones.

Damon, a Harvard graduate, was working as an educational administrator for the state education agency of the District of Columbia when God impressed upon his heart to make a change. God gave him a revelation and confirmed it through a few trust-worthy people. His task, if he accepted, was to start a school. He was eventually given a name for the school - STEAM America. STEAM = Science, Technology, Engineering, the Arts, and Math. (This is a controversial derivative of STEM.)

He did more than tell others what he was

doing; he showed he was serious when he gave up his financial security to follow God. He wrote his letter of resignation and held it for three months until he heard God say, "Proceed."

Everyone knows it takes mature faith to be single and walk away from your paycheck. Can you imagine doing that? It'd be plausible if your spouse were supporting you. You want to know more, right? I asked him a series of questions hoping to show you what it looks like when you open up.

- Where were you in your career when you made this move?

   I was in somewhat of a transition as the decision to create a school officially was made as an educational administrator as opposed to a teacher. It was my first time working in administration and not directly in service to youth.

- Is that where you wanted to be?

   Yes. I was excited to learn more about the entire educational spectrum. It was rewarding, albeit in a different way from the classroom, to be in a position to support schools in their efforts to empower youth.

- Were you ever concerned that you had made a mistake?

   Absolutely, especially when my life

savings was completely depleted, especially when I almost lost my home. I had to encourage myself and look to the Holy Spirit and the Word for strength and motivation. The fear was in leaving a salaried position, not in being the administration of this new project.

- How have you progressed?

    If the measurement of progression is the increased capacity to walk blindly in faith, there has been much progress. This journey has pruned, shaped, and molded me into somewhat of a new creature.

    Both organizations are growing rapidly, which requires continued prayer, fasting, and seeking His counsel to make sure I'm doing my best to be a decent steward of the visions He's given me [to] foster.

You see, there's more to tell about this faith-filled man. He then began a ministry called S.O.C.K.S. *(So Others Can Keep Striding)*. That's a grassroots movement to demonstrate love by supplying socks, and other essential items, to homeless people.

He doesn't need to tell anyone what he's doing unless he's being interviewed or making a pitch for supporters. He lets the work he's doing speak for him. There's more about him a little later.

Things to consider:
Are you willing to let go of everything and follow God? Do you describe yourself as devoted, committed, dedicated or souled out to Him? Are you willing to prove it like Damon did? Are you a student prepared for your next assignment? Can you hear the Teacher knocking?
Knock, knock, knock.

Chapter 6

The Voice

And a voice came to him, "Rise, Peter; kill and eat." But Peter said, "Not so, Lord! For I have never eaten anything common or unclean." And a voice spoke to him again the second time, "What God has cleansed you must not call common." This was done three times. And the object was taken up into heaven again.

Acts 10:13-16

Peter heard this voice in a dream. How many ways have you heard the voice? How many times have you said, "Something told me to...? God is still speaking to us. We have the Bible, which is the history of what was spoken in times past. Rufus M. Jones writes:

...the Bible is the only evidence we have that our God is a *living, revealing, communicating God.* If God ever spoke, He is still speaking.[1]

He goes on to say that we should expect that God would continue to reveal to us His will. Discernment is needed to determine whose voice it is. 1 Corinthians 14:10-11 (KJV) says:

There are, it may be, so many kinds of voices in the world, and none of them is without signification. Therefore, if I know not the meaning of the voice, I shall be unto him that speaketh a barbarian, and he that speaketh shall be a barbarian unto me.

Three times God's voice spoke to Peter in one dream. How many times has it spoken to you? His voice often conflicts with the way you've done things. He will challenge your faith to make you grow. He wants you to trust Him. Peter finally awoke and the rest, as they say, is history. What's your history? Do you have a record of discerning, trusting and obeying God's voice, or are you still struggling in this area?

Peter had a little help in responding to his dream because, as the story goes, three men had come who confirmed what he had seen and heard. Oh, that we should always be so blessed, but we're not. At this point in Peter's life, I believe that he would not have responded without this help because it says in verse 17, "while he doubted." So, as you can see, all of us have had doubts. Nevertheless, we can't keep turning our backs and walking away. God was opening a door to the Gentiles. If Peter hadn't responded, do you think that God would have found someone else to go to Cornelius' house? If you don't follow Him, you may miss His will for your life. Don't assume that you have. Get out of the pit of despair, and call on the name of the Lord.

The Shepherd calls the sheep, and they listen to His voice. Then He "leads them out." There is a big difference between "lead" and push or follow. (Was God trying to use Rhoda to lead Peter into the prayer room?)

The Bible is replete with stories of those who didn't acknowledge His voice, or only partially obeyed, starting with Adam and Eve. We've read about their disobedience and how much it cost them and all of us. Many times our rebellion will take a toll on others as well. I'm sure you can think of several such stories in the scriptures and perhaps your personal lives. I believe everything we do or don't do has an effect on others. That effect might be our bad attitude because we know we messed up and are feeling ashamed, downcast or arrogant. No man is an island, so remember there isn't anything you can do (or refuse to do) concerning the will of God that won't, in some way, have an effect on another person. There is no truth in, "I'm not hurting anybody." Yes, you are in one way or another.

    I was angry with God after dropping out of Nyack College. I tried to go to classes at the temporary location they set up a few blocks away, but that meant walking through the downtown area with that horrific smell; I was afraid of what contaminates were in the air. Also, I had to show my identification whenever a military person requested it. Thank God, that this isn't our norm and I pray it never is. I was already claustrophobic; then one evening, it gripped me so bad while I was walking under scaffolding that I almost laid down on the sidewalk. Instead, I froze. I couldn't move but could hear myself screaming inside my head. If only someone would just grab and hug me before the screams came out. Thank God, the anxiety passed after a few minutes. I realized that day I couldn't go back to New York. I was angry because no one at the school encouraged me to take that semester off; no one at work suggested getting counseling; no one offered any help. In hindsight, no one could.

The Voice

Everyone was reeling from what happened, and almost all of them could have used a little therapy. I wasn't special.

I asked God what was the point of allowing me to attend school for one semester. He knew it had been an almost life-long dream. Why did that have to happen now or ever? My plans were ruined. My roommate was still in North Carolina, far away from the smoke and smells, getting her degree; her plans were moving forward. Of course, there wasn't anywhere in this nation, hardly the world, that didn't feel the devastation that was caused that horrible day. To cap it all off, when I looked to a close family member for comfort I was told that neither my siblings nor I were "college material." *"What!?* That's what you have to say? Where's the encouragement? Where's the, *'It'll be all right; just wait a little while'?* Where's the empathy? I'll answer those questions in another book. (What a story that'll be!) I was devastated. I was seething inside feeling as if a mean joke had been played on me. I told myself, "Oh taste and see, but you can't eat it." I personalized what happened in a very cruel way and, of course, my attitude overflowed and contaminated some friendships I had. I don't want to think about how much it adversely affected my family life.

My anger and the ensuing depression had an effect on my body. My bones seemed to have gone into contortions and caused great pain. Stress can cause physical suffering. From January to August of 2002, I had to have physical therapy because of a slipped disc, upper back, and shoulder pain. I also had carpel tunnel surgery on both hands. The insurance company asked if I had been in a car accident.

Like Peter, I had a dream, the one I mentioned earlier about the building I was working in being destroyed. (That one wasn't destroyed by the attacks; however, I was given permission to tour the company's building in Manhattan that was partially destroyed that day. That too is another story.) I didn't have the help, as Peter received, to properly interpret that dream. I knew my position was being eliminated, but didn't know to take charge, open the door and walk. If I had, I wouldn't have been working in New York at that time. I may not have started school there either.

The truth that I chose to ignore is what God had said earlier. He would teach me what I needed to know. Are you familiar with the story of Balaam, and his ass? In Numbers 22, King Balak sent an offering to the prophet Balaam to come and curse the Israelites for him. The LORD told him not to go, so he refused. King Balak sent a greater gift to reward him if he'd just come and curse these people whom he feared. This time, God gave him permission to go, with instructions to only say what He instructed. As he traveled along the way, the Angel of the Lord stopped him and threatened to kill him if he proceeded. Why, did He do that after giving him permission to go on this journey? The answer may be that God saw his heart. Balaam was, perhaps, looking for a way to collect that great reward by somehow usurping God's authority. God had to put him in check before temptation overtook him. If God had allowed me to follow my heart and earn a degree at that time, I'd have been like those in Genesis 11, who tried to build a wall up to heaven to make a name for themselves. I was already stubborn; being stubborn with knowledge may have made me more like Balaam's ass.

That's enough time spent on gloominess. In God's merciful loving kindness, He allowed me to see that I was *college material*. Even though I said I would never attempt to go to college again, many years later, I did. I earned a degree, and graduated magna cum laude, only in liberal arts. My idea was to earn a doctorate degree in knowledge. No, there's no such thing. I'm satisfied with an Associates, for now.

You all own many secrets of failing to listen to God and follow His instructions, enough to write your own book.

Do you really know when God is speaking or are you just hardheaded? My son said he learned one way to tell the difference. If he hears a suggestion, he knows it's not God. Oh, yes, the devil is always giving suggestions. Whatever he can do, he will, if it causes you to doubt what God said. He will also try to cause confusion about what you heard.

Luther said this about hearing God's voice:

> *I do not know it and I do not understand it, but sounding from above and ringing in my ears, I hear what is beyond the thought of man.*[2]

Others have a problem believing that God is still speaking. Even in Jesus day men preferred to say, "it thundered" (John 12:29), rather than to acknowledge the truth. Scientific research has clouded the minds of many who prefer to examine what God says instead of believing. A.W. Tozer says, the man of God "falls to his knees and whispers, 'God.'" The earthly-minded man bows down too but to, "examine, to search, to find the cause and how of things."[3]

Solomon tells us to *cry out for discernment (Proverbs. 2:3)*. James tells us to ask God for wisdom (James 1:5). Paul tells us to *not be unwise* but know the will of God (Ephesians 5:17. He wouldn't have said that if it wasn't possible to know God's will. Thank God for the written Word, which does still speak to us; yet, God speaks to us in other ways as well. Don't be deceived by letting your impatience, guilt, fear or fleshly desires get in your way. If you're not sure, get counsel from those who are wiser than you are. I'll say it again, folks, you have the final say. I can't imagine telling God, "Well, my pastor said you meant for me to... and he must have been wrong." Blaming someone else didn't work for Adam and it won't work for you or me.

Remember when the nameless prophet from Judah went to prophesy in Bethel? (1 Kings 13) God gave him a message to deliver to King Jeroboam. He also received instructions to return home another way and not to stop to eat or drink. Another prophet sent his sons to catch up with the man and lie that God had said he could come to his house for dinner. Well, he believed this man of God, so he turned back for a morsel of bread. He never made it home. He was eaten by a lion due to his disobedience. Thank God for grace and mercy, and a lion-free neighborhood. Wait, did I just hear a roar?

Let me share a few times when I heard the Voice and responded in the right way.

One such time that I took heed was on Palm Sunday, March 20, 2005. It was the time in the service when the pastor read the scripture that his sermon would come from. He read Mark 11:1-3; he may have read more, but that's all I heard. The words hit me, and I froze. The church could have burned to the ground around me, and I would have sat there without noticing. Those words had me transfixed as they penetrated the very core of my being. They banged on the door of my heart. The particular words from that portion of scripture that mesmerized me were:

> *Ye shall find a colt tied, whereon never man sat; loose him, and bring him. And if any man say unto you, 'Why do ye this?', say ye that the Lord hath need of him.*

Out of this portion, the words that were translated to me were, "*Loose her for the Lord has need of her.*" The revelation that I received was that it was time to let go of everything that hindered me from accepting the call God had on my life. The time was now, no more excuses. I, like Moses, had known for years that I was called to do something for God. I, like Moses, tried to take matters into my own hands. Like Moses, I moved in my own way and time. I, like Moses, was put on the backside of a mountain for a very long time. Those words that day were like my burning bush experience. I became, in a manner of speaking, deaf and mute during the rest of the service. I'm not even sure if I got up to take my offering or if the others on the pew had to step over me. As I look back, I realize I did have help in answering the call that day. At the end of the service, the pastor would always say something like, "The doors of the church are open. If anyone wants to give their life to the Lord or join the church, come forward now." What he asked this day, for the first time I had ever heard, was, "If anyone has been called to serve the Lord, come forth now." What? Why did he say that? I sat for a moment and watched a few others go forth. I was asking God. "What do You want to me do? Surely, not preach". I heard this, "If you don't go up now I will not call you again." I definitely recognized the Voice. I had heard it before when I tried to take over with a "Thanks, God; I got this from here" attitude. I heard it, at least, two other times before that and excitedly told family and friends about it each time. Then fear would take over, and I'd leave the church I was attending when anyone tried to make me open up and accept the call.

I heard the Voice at other times concerning other situations but hadn't heard it for a long time until that day. I understood that there wouldn't be a plan B. I shudder to think what would have happened if I hadn't run to the front of the church that day. I was ready for whatever He wanted of me.

The pastor told the congregation that the following Sunday, which was Easter, all of those who came forward would give a trial sermon. In the African Methodist Episcopal Zion church, each member is assigned a Class Leader. Their function is to assist the pastor with the members, similar to the help Moses received when going through the wilderness. They had the power to approve or reject your request to go forward in the ministry.

Some of those who had stood with me Palm Sunday, in response to the call, didn't show up the next week. I did give my trial sermon and was recommended by the Class Leaders to go forward to receive licensing as the next step in the ordination process. The rest, I'll say again, is history; thank God, it's still being written.

Another time I heard the knock, recognized the voice and opened up was in writing this book. I've wanted to write since grammar school. I did but never had any family or teacher support; mostly because no one was aware that it was a passion. I didn't always write; I couldn't. I would get writers block for years at a time. (The reasons for this may appear in a future book.) Many times, I've read something years after I had written it and couldn't believe that it was mine. I would wonder where my head was at in that season of my life, and how could I get back there. Whether it was poetry, a short story or love letter, I was often amazed.

I was in a children's literature class, and the professor was returning book reports we had written. One, she said she had to read to the class. As I listened, I felt a little jealous and thought, "I wish I could write like that." Then she handed me the paper. It was mine! Again, I asked myself, "Where was I and how can I get back there?" When I read this book, I hope I have the same experience.

I do know that I'm trying to help someone know that hearing and obeying God's voice isn't for entertainment purposes. Read the newspapers, watch the news, look around your neighborhood and even in your church, prophecies are being fulfilled. The world is quickly tumbling out of control, and the Gospel has to be preached to the
You won't likely hear an audible voice speaking to you as you would that of a person, but the Spirit will give witness to your spirit, and you can have an assurance as though you had heard a thundering voice. God isn't answering your prayers

for your gratification; He's calling you to do something valuable; something with far-reaching, eternal results. You have a purpose to fulfill. Don't you hear Him?

Things to consider:

Have you ever been angry with God? Were there any major life-changing events that hindered your walk with Him? Have you given up hope of walking in the fullness of your dreams? Are you afraid to question God?

Knock, knock, knock!

Chapter 7

Come In

Behold I stand at the door and knock: if any man hears my voice, and open the door, I will come in to him, and will sup with him, and he with me.

Revelation 3:20 (KJV)

There's a favorite old hymn that says: *"Tis so sweet to trust in Jesus / just to take Him at His word / just to rest upon His promise / just to know, 'Thus saith the Lord.'"*[1]

Doesn't that sound like the way you want to live your life, by just taking Jesus at His word and resting on His promises? I don't know about you, but I've been guilty of taking parts of His word. What a mess that can become.

Please, allow me to share another story. As they say, "The names have been changed...."

A member of the church, Joan, was in the hospital. God impressed upon my heart to visit her after service this particular Sunday. I would need to ask one of the ladies, Dianne, to let me use her car, which wasn't unusual since my car wasn't working at the time. I had written a little song a few weeks prior that I was sure I would sing to Joan to minister to her. He also impressed upon me (rather strongly), to go alone.

Between Sunday school and the main service, another dear friend, Allison, asked what I was doing after service. We often visited those who were shut-in or hospitalized so of course I told her where I was going. It was still fresh in my mind what I had heard, "Go alone."

Come In

There was an afternoon fellowship the members planned to attend but the church van wasn't going. Diane needed her car, but could spare an hour and a half loan before leaving. As a trustee, she needed time to do bookkeeping. That didn't leave me much time to make this visit. Another elder woman, Ms. Cora, asked me how I was going to get to the second service. I explained that I wasn't and deliberately didn't tell her I was going to the hospital. I suspected she would want to come too. Needless to say, I didn't have to; Allison told her and they had both already determined they were riding with me. Do you know the pain you get in your stomach when you know you've done the wrong thing? I settled it by telling myself I'll run out of the church and leave before Ms. Cora came out. At least, that would eliminate one of these add-ons. I'd be okay with Allison if I can run into the room first before she walks in and do what the Lord had for me to do and everything will work out. Not so! First, Allison had to go to the bathroom; then she had to talk to everyone as she was leaving the church.

I was in the car when Allison got in the back seat. I told her just to shut the door because another driver, who heard me start the car, was looking at me rather impatiently, obviously waiting for the parking space. She asked me to wait a minute because Ms. Cora was on her way out too. By now, I was almost livid, and yelled at her asking, "Why did you tell her where we were going?" All I kept hearing was, "Go alone" ringing in my ear.

I pulled out of the parking space and went around the block to pull up in front of the church. More time wasted. I watched, impatiently, as people were leaving the building, but where was Ms. Cora? Finally, someone came over to tell me that Ms. Cora had fallen down the steps, apparently rushing to catch up with me. They had taken her back inside the sanctuary to see if she was all right. I didn't know what to do. If I waited any longer, I wouldn't have enough time to go before returning the car. Since Ms. Cora was being taken care of I decided to take off.

I was wondering, what service I could render to God with the mood I was in now. What if He's tapping His fingers, looking at me with a scowl on His face, and saying, *"What did I tell you to do?"*

I didn't have any anger left, just the feelings of guilt from being so disobedient. I apologized to Allison, who is always gracious and forgiving. What was done was done, and I'd still have to face God about it when I got home.

When I took Dianne her car keys, she told me Ms. Cora had been taken to the hospital in an ambulance. I was devastated. I tried calling her family to see how she was, but no answer. Finally, I called my pastor's home, hoping he had returned from the afternoon service. He had and had changed his clothes to relax for the evening. He hadn't heard from anyone and assumed they had kept her in the hospital. He got dressed to go back out to check on her. He found that she was still in the emergency room.

I didn't hear anything more until I reached her in the morning. She was home, but still aching from the fall. Thank God, nothing was broken. I profusely apologized for rushing her, then tried to ease my guilt by explaining what happened. I told her if I had been obedient and followed God's clear instructions the entire day would have been better for Cora, Allison, our pastor, and myself. She was very gracious as well. However, my disobedience still caused others to suffer. It was another lesson learned.

Opening the door to let God into our hearts is not always in response to our prayers. Sometimes, God has an assignment for you to carry out. The Holy Spirit isn't a bully. He doesn't force His way on us. He doesn't give us suggestions either; His instructions are clear. Go back to Chapter 5 and read

Damon's story. There's another question he answered for me:

> Where are you in the process of realizing your dream?
>
>> Great question. I ask myself that quite often. Not as far as I'd like to be, but I am assured that the progression of the vision is manifesting according to His divine plan. Additionally, the vision continues to grow. The current picture of what is purposed to manifest is very different from what I thought it would be when I stepped out to begin. It is bigger and has forced me to submit to His will and timing.

This is what happens when your faith is willing to stretch. He was excited about STEAM; still, he followed God to create SOCKS.

I don't know about you, but I'm always praying for God to use me. I tell Him that with my whole heart I'll obey Him. Then, when He asks the simplest thing, I blow it. Admit it; you do too, more often than you care to admit. Leviticus 8:22-23 says:

> *And he brought the second ram, the ram of consecration. Then Aaron and his sons laid their hands on the head of the*

ram, and Moses killed it. Also, he took some of its blood and put it on the tip of Aaron's right ear, on the thumb of his right hand, and on the big toe of his right foot.

The blood was put on the ear that they may hear; it was put on the thumb that they may work; it was put on the great toe that they may walk worthy of the vocation for which they had been called.[2] If you are guilty of hearing, but not taking action, I want you to know that the blood of Jesus cleanses. Repent and turn back to God.

"Rise up, ye women that are at ease; hear my voice, ye careless daughters; give ear unto my speech" (Isaiah 32:9). Carelessness and complacency are thieves that rob us, men and women, of a deeper intimacy with God. When we give ear to *what thus saith the Lord*, our lives are so enriched. As we yield our rights to God, He releases His power in us.

Be determined to live large in Christ and to let His words live large in you. That's what abiding in Him is all about. Haven't you tasted and realized that the Lord is good. Now, eat and be filled by opening the door wide to your heart and welcoming Him in.

I'm so glad that I went forward and began the journey to becoming an ordained minister in the

African Methodist Episcopal Zion Church. I am still awed that He chose me. I thank God for others who had more faith in this call than I did. I also thank God because I didn't have any, "Yea, hath God said," people present at that time in my life to try to cause me to doubt what I heard.

Haven't you heard that Walt Disney was told by an editor that he didn't have enough imagination before he fired him? Have you ever gone to Disney World or Disneyland? What about singer Anita Baker, who was told by a record company that she couldn't sing? She went on to win eight Grammy Awards and was nominated for nine others.

You certainly have a story to tell. As I said before there are many times we can easily recall when we didn't respond to what God said. Take a few minutes and remember the times that you did. Really, at some time, you did hear the knock, recognized the voice and opened the door to your heart. Don't let Satan, our eternal enemy, hold you back by filling your mind with times of disappointments. You probably opened the door when you bought this book. Even if you asked to borrow it, or someone gave it to you to read, I believe it's in response to the knock and the Voice.

It doesn't matter how the knock comes. God will even use your enemy to give you a divine message. He still uses dreams, visions, prophets and ministers. He'll even use billboards and songs. Take the challenge to listen for the knock. Rhoda listening and she heard.

Its written in Luke 6:46, "But why do you call Me 'Lord, Lord,' and not do the things which I say?" What's going to be your answer to this question? He may ask you one of these questions:

1. Didn't you trust Me?
2. Didn't you hear Me?
3. Didn't you recognize My voice?
4. Why were you afraid?
5. Whom did you choose to follow instead of Me?

I don't want to have those questions asked of me. I don't want them to be asked of you either. What are you going to do to avoid them? Write todays date down in your Bible, on your calendar, your phone or IPad and go back every week or so and see if you would have had any reason to answer those questions. Every time you check for entries, do a self-examination to see if you're progressing in preparing to open your heart to whatever God says. According to Christian author Stephen F. Winward:

Progress in holiness can best be measured not by the length of time we spend in prayer, not by the number of times we go to church, not by the amount of money we contribute to God's work, not by the range and depth of our knowledge of the Bible, but rather by the quality of our personal relationships. [3]

Our personal relationship is determined by our obedience. Consistency determines our destiny. We need to respond to the promptings of the Holy Spirit and allow Him to penetrate our hearts to take us to the place beyond being *happy* that we heard from Him to the place where we open up and allow all the possibilities He presents us with to be carried out in our lives.

Several times I had been inspired, one way or another, to write. My first attempt was to start a magazine titled, "From the Cross to the Crown." That was around 1997. I had a group of ladies working with me, and I had gotten them just as excited as I was about this revelation. They were convinced that I had what it took to do this. However, my inexperience, lack of education and abundance of fear stopped me. It didn't take much to accept the doubts that I wasn't qualified to take on such a project.

Oh, did I mention I thought God was to follow me in this undertaking, always looking back over my shoulder to see if He was still there. Nope, He wasn't but I was sure He'd catch up. What foolishness.

Come In

"Yes, tis sweet to trust in Jesus, just from sin and self to cease, just from Jesus simply taking, life and rest, and joy and peace."

A few years later, I went to one of T.D. Jakes', "Woman, Thou Art Loosed" conferences in Atlanta. I was so pumped by that I told one of the conference workers that the following year I'd be back with my magazine. Over and over again through a twenty-year period whenever I would hear that knock to write I would share my vision and enthusiasm, yet, somehow let doubt, fear, financial insufficiencies, low self-esteem, insecurities, even my battle with my weight keep me from opening that door. (I couldn't do a book tour if I was ashamed of my appearance. What would I wear to fuel my confidence?)

I recognized that it was God calling me to do this; and I didn't have any doubt about that. I hadn't actually prayed about becoming a writer, but it was a desire planted in me from the days of my youth. As I said before I was always writing little poems or short stories.

As the years went on I felt so foolish, for repeating myself, "Yes, I'm finally going to get that book out; read these few pages and tell me what you think." I just couldn't keep the joy that would come over me to myself. Sometimes, I would have a dream, or words would come to me, and I would write them down.

One time, I attended a service and answered the altar call for prayer for the family. I wanted the evangelist to pray for my son. Each person would give her a name or specific situation to pray about. When she got to me, she said, "All I see is writing. What's all this about writing?" Then she said a prayer and walked to the next person in line. I stood there a minute wondering why didn't she ask me whom in my family I wanted prayer for. For several days, I was in a daze asking God, "What do You want me to do?" I didn't want to get excited again, start writing again, and stop again. This was making me feel more and more like a failure. Again, He knew I needed a degree in journalism or, at least, English to do what He required of me. How could He keep teasing me like that?

An often quoted scripture is Romans 4:17,"*(As it is written, I have made thee a father of many nations,) before him whom he believed, even God, who quickeneth the dead, and calleth those things which be not as though they were.*" God called the world into existence. It went from a "*be not*" state, to "*there it is.*" I've tried to call things into existence without success. I called those things I wanted while facing east, then west, even north, then south. I tried calling things into existence while on my knees while facing the wall, and while walking through Macy's; nothing happened, (I'll address this again later). I believe in confessing the scriptures over my life and definitely use them in prayer. However, some things I believe are in the realm of possibility for God alone.

Was the vision to be a writer waiting for the appointed time? You can answer that however you'd like.

Things to consider:

There's only one point in sharing so much of my life with you. That point was to help you consider why you haven't fulfilled your God-given dreams and desires. Perhaps you've never had experiences like mine, and that's alright. Nevertheless, you may have had something that kept holding you back. I hope you've been stirred up to find out what that was and even how to get it out of your way.

Time is quickly passing away. It's time to move out of the ordinary and into the extraordinary life God has prepared for you.

Open the door and embrace the opportunities that will lead to a richer life.

Epilogue

I'm not Rhoda!

That's my declaration.

Normally, when a guest comes to your house, you open the door and, make a motion with your hand, which welcomes them in. Then you allow them to walk ahead of you into the living area. The only time I'll go first is when I'm trying to clear a walking path, or remove "stuff" from the sofa so they can sit. Follow Jesus when you open the door. Don't worry about being untidy. He'll take care of all that for you. He's not coming in to sit. There's work for you to do.

When you open the door, you may not *see* the manifestation of what God has prepared, or is preparing for you. We walk by faith, not by sight. Read the story of Elijah in 1 Kings 17:8-16. God told him that He had prepared a widow to feed him during a drought, which brought about a famine as well. He went to the widow of Zarephath, as instructed. She explained that she only had enough provisions to prepare a final meal for herself, and her son before they would die. Elijah didn't doubt what God had said, even though in the natural he had every reason to do so. This is where you confess and call things into existence. In verse 14 he told this woman, "For thus says the LORD God of Israel: 'The bin of flour shall not be used up, nor shall the jar of oil run dry, until the day the LORD sends rain on the earth.'" His faith stood firm on what God had spoken, not on what he heard from this woman.

What has God told you? Did He tell you to start a business, move to Guyana, leave your employment to write a book, give away your deliciously baked goods to a shelter, go into ministry or something else? Have you ever gone to your pastor, supervisor or spouse and shared your desire? If you haven't, do so, quickly. If the reply is, "No", or "That's a great idea. I'm going to let my wife do that." (Or some other person.) What will you do? Remember to STOP (chapter 3). If you know God called you to a ministry and you're not allowed to work it out in the church, or place of employment, find out if you can fulfill your desire in the community. Talk to community leaders, school administrators or perhaps now is the time to present it to your friends. You may be called to start a movement with only two or three people. If your spouse is the hindering agent, pray. God is ready to make a way for His will to be done. Whatever it is, take the first step, and follow Him into your purpose.

My prayer is that you (yes, **you**), are reading this book because God wants you to follow Him, now! He's been working to build you up to the place where you will step out onto the water. If you keep your eyes on Him, you won't drown. If you follow Him, you won't get lost in the wilderness.

If you really know that you've missed the boat, and you're not an Abraham, Sarah or Moses, then please know that you still have a purpose. Mentor, encourage or earnestly pray for someone who is pressing forward.

Grateful isn't a strong enough word to describe the appreciation I have for those who encouraged, supported and prayed for me. I praise God for His persistence to bring this project to fruition. This is one of many hurdles I have had to overcome. There are other missions and ministries I have to give birth to.

It's painful to admit that I'm still struggling with my will. However, I don't take as long as I once did to open my heart when I recognize that it's God knocking. First, I take the time to meditate on what I've heard. Next, I search the scriptures for support. When necessary, I seek godly counsel from two or three. 2 Corinthians 13:1 is my support for this - *"By the mouth of two or three witnesses every word shall be established."*

There's a great song titled, *Let Him In,*[1] written by J.B. Atchinson, that wraps this all up. The song says, "There's a Stranger at the door; let Him in." Too often, we act as if God is a stranger. We peek through the peephole of our souls and consider if we'll open the door or not. Sometimes, we aren't even conscious of what we're doing. Don't be like Rhoda. Open up the door. The Spirit of God is knocking; let Him in, then follow Him to fulfill your purpose.

Let Him In

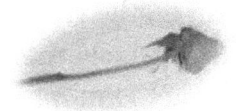

Let Him In

There's a Stranger at the door,
Let Him in;
He has been there oft before,
Let Him in;
Let Him in, ere He is gone,
Let Him in, the Holy One,
Jesus Christ, the Father's Son,
Let Him in.

Open now to Him your heart,
Let Him in;
If you wait He will depart,
Let Him in;
Let Him in, He is your Friend,
He your soul will sure defend,
He will keep you to the end,
Let Him in.

Hear you now His loving voice?
Let Him in;
Now, oh, now make Him your choice,
Let Him in;
He is standing at your door,
Joy to you He will restore,
And His name you will adore,
Let Him in.

Now admit the heav'nly Guest,
Let Him in;
He will make for you a feast,
Let Him in;
He will speak your sins forgiv'n.
And when earth ties all are riv'n,
Comfort, rest, you will be giv'n,
Let Him in.

ENDNOTES

Prologue
[1] Isaiah 30:21
[2] www.brainyquote.com/quotes/authors/b/benjamin_franklin.html.
[3] John 10:1-3

Chapter 1
[1] "Acts." The NIV Matthew Henry Commentary in One Volume. Ed. Leslie F. Church and Gerald W. Peterman. Broad Oak Edition ed. Michigan: Zondervan, 1992. 491. Print.
[2] Blount, Brian K., Cain Hope. Felder, Clarice Jannette Martin, and Emerson B. Powery. "The Acts of the Apostles." True to Our Native Land: An African American New Testament Commentary. Minneapolis: Fortress, 2007. 232. Print.
[3] www.goodreads.com/author/quotes/66179.Mark_Batterson.

Chapter 2
[1] Jones, Rufus M. *A Call to What Is Vital*. New York: Macmillan, 1948. 42. Print.
[2] Acts." The NIV Matthew Henry Commentary in One Volume. Ed. Leslie F. Church and Gerald W. Peterman. Broad Oak Edition ed. Michigan: Zondervan, 1992. 491. Print.
[3] Psalm 138:2, 37:25, Philippians 4:19
[4] Order My Steps, Glen Burleigh, 1991. Lyrics
[5] "Revelation Is Not Enough." *God still Speaks: Are we Listening*. Cross Reach, 2014. Loc. 167 of 635. Digital
[6] Jeremiah, David. "Defeat: The Fear of Failure." *What Are You Afraid Of?: Facing Down Your Fears With Faith*. Carol Stream: Tyndale House, 2013. 87-90. Print
[7] Exodus 2:11-15

[8]"Malachi." The NIV Matthew Henry Commentary in One Volume. Ed. Leslie F. Church and Gerald W. Peterman. Broad Oak Edition ed. Michigan: Zondervan, 1992. 1233. Print.

[9]Number 9:15-23

Chapter 3

[1]Genesis 3:1

[2]Harper, Douglas. "Online Etymology Dictionary."Online Etymology Dictionary.

Chapter 4

[1]Packer, J. I., Merrill C. Tenney, and William White. "Plants and Herbs." *Nelson's Illustrated Encyclopedia of Bible Facts.* Nashville: T. Nelson, 1995. 245-46, 260. Print.

[2]Ibid p. 245

[3]Wilkinson, Bruce, and David Kopp. "The Best Good News." *Secrets of the Vine: Breaking Through to Abundance.* Sisters, OR.: Multnomah, 2001. 29-41. Print

[4] www.deeprootsathome.com/pruning-a-grapevine-bountiful-fruit.

Chapter 6

[1]Jones, Rufus M. *A Call to What Is Vital.* New York: Macmillan, 1948. 65. Print.

[2]Ibid p. iii

[3]"The speaking Voice". God Still Speaks: Are We Listening. Cross Reach, 2014. Loc. 248-253. Digital

Chapter 7

[1] Stead, Louisa M. R., and William J. Kirkpatrick. "Tis So Sweet to Trust in Jesus." *The New National Baptist Hymnal.* Nashville: National Baptist Board, 1977. N. hymn 196. Print.

[2]Ryrie, Charles Caldwell. "Exodus 29:1-37." The Ryrie Study Bible: King James Version: Chicago: Moody, 1978. 137. Print.

[3]Winward, Stephen F. "Beliefnet's Inspirational Quotes". *Beliefnet.com*. Web.

Epilogue
[1] Atchinson, J. B. "Let Him In." *Hymnary.org*.

Recommended Reading:

"*Under Cover: The Promise of Protection Under His Authority*", by John Bevere

"*Pain Drives Change*", by Damon Stoddard

"*Deep & Wide*" by Andy Stanley

About the Author

Rev. Jacqueline Withers is an ordained Deacon in the African Methodist Episcopal Zion Church. She is an Associate Pastor at Peoples AME Zion Church in Carteret, NJ, currently serving under the Rev. Charles Washington.

She preaches regularly in her local church, as an invited speaker in other area churches and weekly for Day Start, a weekday conference call ministry created by Rev. Mack Brandon.

She is the mother of two children, Jonathan and Olivia, and grandmother of five.

She has written skits, and songs used for Vacation Bible School, Bible study and work-related promotions, as well as newsletters, and tracks for evangelism. She also wrote a play titled "Your Slip is Showing." Her first published work was a poem titled "I Want" printed in "With Hearts Ablaze", by the International Library of Poetry, in 2003.

She spends time volunteering for Garden State Episcopal CDC, a homeless advocacy agency in New Jersey.

Her two favorite scriptures are:

> Psalm 27:13 – *"I had fainted, unless I had believed to see the goodness of the LORD in the land of the living."*
> Isaiah 38:17 – *"Behold, for peace I had great bitterness: but thou hast in love to my soul delivered it from the pit of corruption: for thou hast cast all my sins behind thy back."*

She can be contacted at rhodaopenup@gmail.com

Look for the next book, to be released soon, by Rev. J. Withers:

- *"I'm Not Rhoda*: Prayer Journal"